Baby's Buddy
Amigurumi

Life is more fun with a special buddy and a warm blanket! For any of these toys you choose to make, there is a striped car seat blanket on page 22 that you can color-coordinate to go with it.

CONTENTS

LEISURE ARTS, INC. • Maumelle, Arkansas

ELEPHANT

Finished Size: Approximately 7" (18 cm) tall (seated)

SHOPPING LIST

YARN

(Medium Weight) MEDIUM 4

- ☐ Light Lavender - 285 yards (261 meters)
- ☐ White - 50 yards (45.5 meters)

CROCHET HOOKS

- ☐ Size E (3.5 mm) for Elephant
- ☐ Size H (5 mm) for Diaper **or** size needed for gauge

ADDITIONAL SUPPLIES

- ☐ Safety pin
- ☐ White felt - 6" (15 cm) square
- ☐ White embroidery floss
- ☐ ¾" (19 mm) Button
- ☐ Sewing needle
- ☐ Yarn needle
- ☐ Polyester fiberfill
- ☐ 10.5 mm black safety eyes - 2 (Please take caution if the toy is for a child that is at risk of choking. See Safety, page 44.)

GAUGE INFORMATION

Gauge for the elephant is **not** of great importance as long as your crochet fabric is very dense ***(see Gauge, page 43)***.

STITCH GUIDE

SINGLE CROCHET 2 TOGETHER
(abbreviated sc2tog)
Pull up a loop in each of next 2 sc, YO and draw through all 3 loops on hook (**counts as one sc**).

HEAD

Rnd 1 (Right side)**:** Beginning at trunk, with Light Lavender and leaving a long end for sewing, make an adjustable loop to form a ring ***(Figs. 1a-d, page 44)***; work 6 sc in ring; do **not** join, place marker to indicate beginning of rnd ***(see Markers, page 45)***.

Rnds 2-6: Sc in each sc around.

Rnd 7: (Sc in next sc, 2 sc in next sc) around: 9 sc.

Rnd 8: (Sc in next 2 sc, 2 sc in next sc) around: 12 sc.

Rnd 9: Sc in each sc around; slip the loop from the hook onto a safety pin to prevent the trunk from unraveling while you shape it.

Insert the long end through a st on Rnd 8 ***(Photo 1)*** and pull the yarn until the Trunk curves ***(Photo 2)***; secure the yarn end.

Photo 1

Photo 2

Rnd 10: Slip loop from safety pin onto crochet hook; sc in each sc around.

Rnd 11: Sc in each sc around.

Rnd 12: (Sc in next 2 sc, 2 sc in next sc) around: 16 sc.

Rnds 13 and 14: (Sc in next 3 sc, 2 sc in next sc) around: 25 sc.

Rnd 15: (Sc in next 4 sc, 2 sc in next sc) around: 30 sc.

Rnd 16: (Sc in next 5 sc, 2 sc in next sc) around: 35 sc.

Rnds 17-19: Sc in each sc around.

Rnd 20: (Sc in next 6 sc, 2 sc in next sc) around: 40 sc.

Rnd 21: (Sc in next 7 sc, 2 sc in next sc) around: 45 sc.

Rnd 22: (Sc in next 8 sc, 2 sc in next sc) around: 50 sc.

Rnd 23: (Sc in next 9 sc, 2 sc in next sc) around: 55 sc.

Note: The loop can be slipped from the hook onto safety pin while attaching the eyes.

Use photos as guides for placement of all pieces. See Tips, page 44, for important information on safety, stuffing, and yarn ends.

Attach safety eyes to Rnd 17 of Head, spacing the posts approximately 9 sc apart centered on each side of the Trunk ***(Photos 3 & 4)***.

Rnds 24-27: Sc in each sc around.

Rnd 28: (Sc in next 9 sc, sc2tog) around: 50 sc.

Rnd 29: (Sc in next 8 sc, sc2tog) around: 45 sc.

Photo 3

Photo 4

Rnd 30: (Sc in next 7 sc, sc2tog) around: 40 sc.

Rnd 31: (Sc in next 6 sc, sc2tog) around: 35 sc.

Rnd 32: (Sc in next 5 sc, sc2tog) around: 30 sc.

Rnd 33: (Sc in next 4 sc, sc2tog) around: 25 sc.

Rnd 34: (Sc in next 3 sc, sc2tog) around: 20 sc.

Stuff Head with polyester fiberfill leaving the trunk unstuffed.

Rnd 35: (Sc in next 2 sc, sc2tog) around: 15 sc.

Rnd 36: (Sc in next sc, sc2tog) around: 10 sc.

Rnd 37: Sc2tog around; slip st in next sc, finish off leaving a long end for sewing: 5 sc.

Weave yarn end through sts on last rnd to close ***(Fig. 4, page 46)***; secure yarn, then insert it through the Head and out to where it will be attached to the Body; do **not** cut yarn.

EAR (Make 2)

With Light Lavender, ch 11.

Row 1: Sc in second ch from hook and in each ch across: 10 sc.

Rows 2-9: Ch 1, turn; skip first sc, sc in each remaining sc across: 2 sc.

Finish off leaving a long end for sewing.

HEAD ASSEMBLY

Use whipstitch ***(Figs. 5a & b, page 46)*** for the method of sewing to join the pieces together.

Using the Ears as guides, cut 2 pieces of felt slightly smaller than the Ears.

Using embroidery floss and sewing needle, sew felt pieces in place ***(Photo 5)***.

Photo 5

Using long yarn ends and yarn needle, sew end of rows on Ears diagonally across the side of the Head. Insert the yarn ends through the Head and out near the other yarn end ***(Photo 6)***; do **not** cut yarn.

Photo 6

Tie all strands together, then hide all but one yarn end in Head.

BODY

Rnd 1 (Right side)**:** With Light Lavender, make an adjustable loop to form a ring; work 6 sc in ring; do **not** join, place marker.

Rnd 2: 2 Sc in each sc around: 12 sc.

Rnd 3: (Sc in next sc, 2 sc in next sc) around: 18 sc.

Rnd 4: (Sc in next 2 sc, 2 sc in next sc) around: 24 sc.

Rnd 5: (Sc in next 3 sc, 2 sc in next sc) around: 30 sc.

Rnd 6: (Sc in next 4 sc, 2 sc in next sc) around: 36 sc.

Rnd 7: (Sc in next 5 sc, 2 sc in next sc) around: 42 sc.

Rnd 8: (Sc in next 6 sc, 2 sc in next sc) around: 48 sc.

Rnd 9: (Sc in next 7 sc, 2 sc in next sc) around: 54 sc.

Rnd 10: (Sc in next 8 sc, 2 sc in next sc) around: 60 sc.

Rnd 11: (Sc in next 9 sc, 2 sc in next sc) around: 66 sc.

Rnd 12: (Sc in next 10 sc, 2 sc in next sc) around: 72 sc.

Rnds 13-15: Sc in each sc around.

Rnd 16: (Sc in next 10 sc, sc2tog) around: 66 sc.

Rnd 17: Sc in each sc around.

Rnd 18: (Sc in next 9 sc, sc2tog) around: 60 sc.

Rnd 19: Sc in each sc around.

Rnd 20: (Sc in next 8 sc, sc2tog) around: 54 sc.

Rnd 21: Sc in each sc around.

Rnd 22: (Sc in next 7 sc, sc2tog) around: 48 sc.

Rnds 23-27: Sc in each sc around.

Rnd 28: (Sc in next 6 sc, sc2tog) around: 42 sc.

Rnd 29: Sc in each sc around.

Rnd 30: (Sc in next 5 sc, sc2tog) around: 36 sc.

Rnd 31: Sc in each sc around.

Rnd 32: (Sc in next 4 sc, sc2tog) around: 30 sc.

Rnd 33: Sc in each sc around.

Stuff Body with polyester fiberfill.

Rnd 34: (Sc in next 3 sc, sc2tog) around: 24 sc.

Rnd 35: Sc in each sc around.

Rnd 36: (Sc in next 2 sc, sc2tog) around: 18 sc.

Rnd 37: (Sc in next sc, sc2tog) around: 12 sc.

Rnd 38: Sc2tog around; slip st in next sc, finish off leaving a long end: 6 sc.

LEG (Make 2)

Work same as Body, page 5, through Rnd 6: 36 sc.

Rnds 7 and 8: Sc in each sc around.

Rnd 9: (Sc in next 4 sc, sc2tog) around: 30 sc.

Rnd 10: (Sc in next 3 sc, sc2tog) around: 24 sc.

Rnd 11: Sc in next 16 sc, sc2tog 4 times: 20 sc.

Rnd 12: Sc in next 12 sc, sc2tog 4 times: 16 sc.

Rnds 13-20: Sc in each sc around.

Slip st in next sc, finish off leaving a long end for sewing.

Stuff Leg with polyester fiberfill.

ARM (Make 2)

Work same as Body, page 5, through Rnd 5: 30 sc.

Rnds 6 and 7: Sc in each sc around.

Rnd 8: (Sc in next 3 sc, sc2tog) around: 24 sc.

Rnd 9: Sc in each sc around.

Rnd 10: (Sc in next 2 sc, sc2tog) around: 18 sc.

Rnd 11: Sc in each sc around.

Rnd 12: (Sc in next sc, sc2tog) around: 12 sc.

Stuff Arm with polyester fiberfill as you work.

Rnds 13-31: Sc in each sc around.

Rnd 32: Sc2tog around; slip st in next sc, finish off leaving a long end for sewing: 6 sc.

BODY ASSEMBLY

Using the bottom of the Legs as guides, cut 2 pieces of felt to cover Rnds 1-5.

Using embroidery floss and sewing needle, sew felt pieces in place.

Flatten last rnd of Legs with the shaping pointing up and sew closed. Sew Legs to Rnd 10 of the Body at an angle approximately 10 sc apart. Insert the yarn ends through the Body and out the neck; do **not** cut yarn.

Flatten last rnd of Arms and sew closed. Sew Arms to Body on the third rnd from the top. Insert the yarn ends through the Body and out the neck; do **not** cut yarn.

TAIL

Cut 3, 10" (25.5 cm) pieces of Light Lavender. Hold pieces together and tie an overhand knot approximately 1" (2.5 cm) from one end. Braid the strands until the Tail measures 1" (2.5 cm) long, then knot the end. Using one strand, sew the braid to Rnd 12 at center back of the Body. Insert the yarn ends through the Body and out the neck; do **not** cut yarn. Fray the loose ends of the Tail.

Tie all strands together at the neck, then hide all yarn ends in the Body.

Sew Head to Body, sewing around the edge 3 times; secure and hide yarn ends.

DIAPER

Gauge: 8 sc and 10 rows = 2" (5 cm)
Gauge Swatch: 2" (5 cm) square
With White, ch 9.
Row 1: Sc in second ch from hook and in each ch across: 8 sc.
Rows 2-10: Ch 1, turn; sc in each sc across.
Finish off.

Note: Because of the differences in stitch tension and how tightly you stuffed your elephant, the number of chains may need to be adjusted to fit your elephant. The chain needs to reach around the belly and overlap 1" (2.5 cm). The stitch counts will change accordingly.

With White, ch 51.

Row 1: Sc in second ch from hook and in each ch across: 50 sc.

Row 2: Ch 1, turn; sc in each sc across.

Row 3: Ch 1, turn; sc in first 2 sc, ch 2, skip next 2 sc (**buttonhole made**), sc in each sc across to last 4 sc, ch 2, skip next 2 sc (**buttonhole made**), sc in last 2 sc: 46 sc and 2 ch-2 sps.

Row 4: Ch 1, turn; sc in each sc and in each ch across: 50 sc.

Row 5: Ch 1, turn; sc in each sc across.

Row 6: Turn; slip st in first 5 sc, sc in each sc across to last 5 sc, leave remaining sc unworked: 40 sc and 5 slip sts.

Row 7: Turn; skip first sc, sc in each sc across to last 7 sts, sc2tog, leave last 5 slip sts unworked: 38 sc.

Rows 8-10: Turn; skip first sc, sc in each sc across to last 2 sc, sc2tog: 32 sc.

Rows 11-14: Turn; skip first sc, sc in each sc across to last 3 sc, sc2tog, leave last sc unworked: 20 sc.

Rows 15-20: Turn; skip first sc, sc in each sc across to last 2 sc, sc2tog: 8 sc.

Rows 21-23: Ch 1, turn; sc in each sc across.

Row 24: Ch 1, turn; 2 sc in first sc, sc each sc across to last sc, 2 sc in last sc: 10 sc.

Rows 25-29: Ch 1, turn; sc in each sc across.

Finish off.

Using embroidery floss and sewing needle, sew button to center of third row from the end. Overlap flaps and place both buttonholes over the button ***(Photo 7)***.

Photo 7

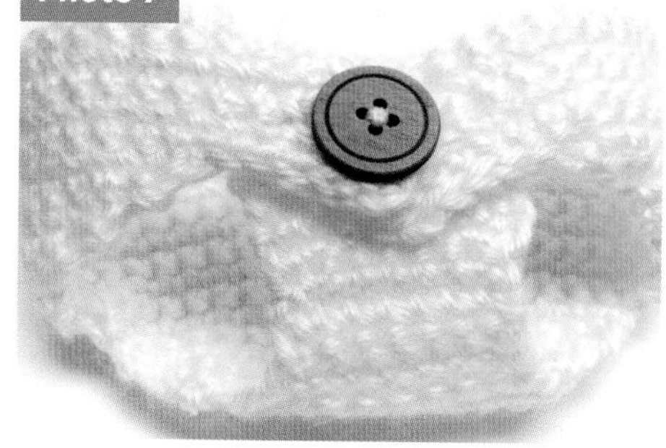

Put the Diaper on Elephant, pulling the Tail through a stitch.

T-REX

Finished Size: Approximately 8½" (21.5 cm) tall

SHOPPING LIST

YARN

(Light Weight) LIGHT 3

- ☐ Main Color (Blue or Lavender) - 140 yards (128 meters)

(Medium Weight) MEDIUM 4

- ☐ Contrasting Color
  Boy (Light Blue) - 21 yards (19 meters)
  Girl (Light Lavender) - 12 yards (11 meters)

CROCHET HOOK

- ☐ Size E (3.5 mm)

ADDITIONAL SUPPLIES

- ☐ Safety pin - for optional marker
- ☐ Black embroidery floss
- ☐ Yarn and tapestry needles
- ☐ Polyester fiberfill

GAUGE INFORMATION

Gauge for the T-Rex is **not** of great importance as long as your crochet fabric is very dense ***(see Gauge, page 43)***.

STITCH GUIDE

SINGLE CROCHET 2 TOGETHER
(abbreviated sc2tog)
Pull up a loop in each of next 2 sc, YO and draw through all 3 loops on hook **(counts as one sc)**.

FRONT POST SINGLE CROCHET
(abbreviated FPsc)
Insert hook from **front** to **back** around post of st indicated ***(Fig. A)***, YO and pull up a loop, YO and draw through both loops on hook.

Fig. A

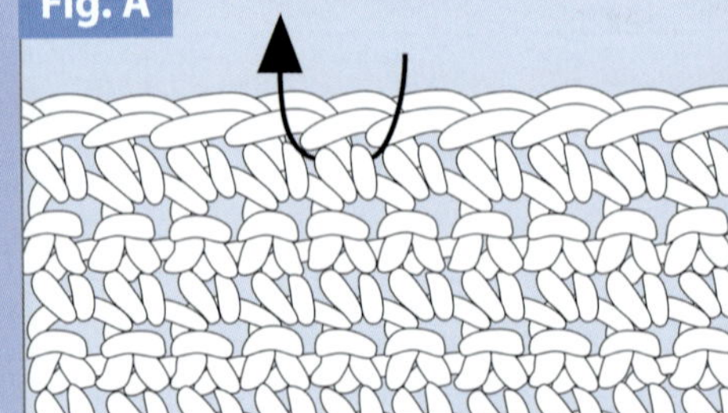

HEAD

Rnd 1 (Right side)**:** With Main Color, make an adjustable loop to form a ring ***(Figs. 1a-d, page 44)***; work 6 sc in ring; do **not** join, place marker to indicate beginning of rnd ***(see Markers, page 45)***.

Rnd 2: 2 Sc in each sc around: 12 sc.

Rnd 3: (Sc in next sc, 2 sc in next sc) around: 18 sc.

Rnd 4: (Sc in next 2 sc, 2 sc in next sc) around: 24 sc.

Rnd 5: (Sc in next 3 sc, 2 sc in next sc) around: 30 sc.

Rnds 6-8: Sc in each sc around.

Rnd 9: (Sc in next sc, 2 sc in next sc) 3 times, sc in each sc around: 33 sc.

Rnd 10: (Sc in next 2 sc, 2 sc in next sc) twice, sc in next sc, 2 sc in next sc, sc in each sc around: 36 sc.

Rnds 11-13: Sc in each sc around.

Rnd 14: (Sc in next 5 sc, 2 sc in next sc) around: 42 sc.

Rnd 15: Sc in next 4 sc, 2 sc in next sc, (sc in next 2 sc, 2 sc in next sc) twice, sc in next 14 sc, sc2tog, (sc in next sc, sc2tog) twice, sc in next 9 sc: 42 sc.

Place marker or safety pin around the center decrease made on Rnd 15 to indicate bottom of Head and for Body placement.

Rnd 16: Sc in next 5 sc, 2 sc in next sc, sc in next 2 sc, 2 sc in next sc, sc in next 3 sc, 2 sc in next sc, sc in each sc around: 45 sc.

Rnd 17: Sc in next 6 sc, sc2tog, (sc in next 3 sc, sc2tog) twice, sc in each sc around: 42 sc.

Rnd 18: Sc in next 7 sc, sc2tog, (sc in next 2 sc, sc2tog) twice, sc in each sc around: 39 sc.

Rnd 19: Sc in next 5 sc, sc2tog, sc in next 2 sc, sc2tog, sc in next sc, sc2tog, sc in each sc around: 36 sc.

Rnd 20: Sc in each sc around.

Rnd 21: (Sc in next 4 sc, sc2tog) around: 30 sc.

Rnd 22: (Sc in next 3 sc, sc2tog) around: 24 sc.

Rnd 23: (Sc in next 2 sc, sc2tog) around: 18 sc.

Stuff Body with polyester fiberfill.

Rnd 24: (Sc in next sc, sc2tog) around: 12 sc.

Rnd 25: Sc2tog around; slip st in next sc, finish off leaving a long end for sewing: 6 sc.

Weave yarn end through the sts on the last rnd to close ***(Fig. 4, page 46)***; secure yarn, then insert it through the Head and out where you marked the center decrease on Rnd 15 ***(Photo 1)***; do **not** cut yarn.

Photo 1

BOY'S HAT

With Contrasting Color, work same as Head, page 8, through Rnd 8: 30 sc.

Rnd 9: (Sc in next 4 sc, 2 sc in next sc) around: 36 sc.

BRIM

Row 1: Work FPsc around each of next 11 sc, leave remaining sc unworked: 11 FPsc.

Row 2: Ch 1, turn; sc in each st across.

Row 3: Ch 1, turn; skip first sc, sc in each sc across: 10 sc.

Edging Rnd: Ch 1, turn; skip first sc, sc in each sc across, sc in end of next 2 rows on Brim and in unworked sc on Rnd 9, sc in end of next 2 rows on Brim; join with slip st to first sc, finish off leaving a long end for sewing ***(Photo 2)***.

Photo 2

GIRL'S BOW

With Contrasting Color, ch 21.

Row 1: Sc in second ch from hook and in each ch across: 20 sc.

Rows 2-6: Ch 1, turn; sc in each sc across.

Finish off leaving a long end for sewing.

Sew the end of rows together forming a circle. Flatten the circle with the seam at the center. Wind the yarn around the seam several times ***(Photo 3)*** and secure yarn; do **not** cut yarn.

Photo 3

HEAD ASSEMBLY

Use photos as guides for placement of all pieces. See Tips, page 44, for important information on safety, stuffing, and yarn ends.

Mark the placement of the eyes on Rnd 10, 12 sts apart.

With Black embroidery floss, insert the needle near the yarn end on the Head and back out at one marked stitch. Embroider the first eye across Rnds 10 and 11 using satin stitch ***(Fig. 7b, page 46)***. Pinch the area between the eyes together to form a bridge and insert the needle through the Head to the other marked stitch, and pull tight to form an indentation. Embroider the second eye in same manner.
Finish by pushing the needle back through the Head and out near the other floss end ***(Photo 4)***. Knot the two ends together, then hide the ends.

Photo 4

Use whipstitch ***(Figs. 5a & b, page 46)*** for the method of sewing to join the pieces together.

Photo 5

Photo 6

For the Boy

Sew the Hat to the top of the Head, stuffing before closing ***(Photos 5 & 6)***; do **not** cut yarn.

For the Girl

Sew the Bow to the side of the Head, 7 rounds above one eye; do **not** cut yarn.

Both Designs

Finish by pushing the needle back through the Head and out near the other yarn end. Tie both strands together, then hide the Hat or Bow yarn end in Head.

BODY

Rnd 1 (Right side)**:** With Main Color, make an adjustable loop to form a ring; work 6 sc in ring; do **not** join, place marker.

Rnd 2: 2 Sc in each sc around: 12 sc.

Rnd 3: (Sc in next sc, 2 sc in next sc) around: 18 sc.

Rnd 4: (Sc in next 2 sc, 2 sc in next sc) around: 24 sc.

Rnd 5: (Sc in next 3 sc, 2 sc in next sc) around: 30 sc.

Rnd 6: (Sc in next 4 sc, 2 sc in next sc) around: 36 sc.

Rnd 7: (Sc in next 5 sc, 2 sc in next sc) around: 42 sc.

Rnd 8: (Sc in next 6 sc, 2 sc in next sc) around: 48 sc.

Rnds 9 and 10: Sc in each sc around.

Rnd 11: (Sc in next 6 sc, sc2tog) around: 42 sc.

Rnd 12: Sc in each sc around.

Rnd 13: (Sc in next 5 sc, sc2tog) around: 36 sc.

Rnd 14: Sc in each sc around.

Rnd 15: (Sc in next 4 sc, sc2tog) around: 30 sc.

Rnds 16-21: Sc in each sc around.

Rnd 22: (Sc in next 3 sc, sc2tog) around: 24 sc.

Rnd 23: Sc in each sc around.

Rnd 24: (Sc in next 2 sc, sc2tog) around: 18 sc.

Rnd 25: Sc in each sc around.

Stuff Body with polyester fiberfill.

Rnd 26: (Sc in next sc, sc2tog) around: 12 sc.

Rnd 27: Sc in each sc around.

Rnd 28: Sc2tog around; slip st in next sc, finish off leaving a long end: 6 sc.

LEG (Make 2)

Leaving a long end for sewing, work same as Body, page 11, through Rnd 5: 30 sc.

Rnd 6: Sc in each sc around.

Rnd 7: (Sc in next 3 sc, sc2tog) around: 24 sc.

Rnd 8: Sc in each sc around.

Rnd 9: (Sc in next 2 sc, sc2tog) around: 18 sc.

Rnd 10: Sc in each sc around.

Stuff Leg with polyester fiberfill.

Rnd 11: (Sc in next sc, sc2tog) around: 12 sc.

Rnds 12 and 13: Sc in each sc around.

Rnd 14: (Sc in next sc, 2 sc in next sc) 3 times, sc2tog 3 times: 12 sc.

Place marker around the center decrease to mark back of ankle.

Rnd 15: Sc in each sc around.

Rnds 16 and 17: (Sc in next sc, 2 sc in next sc) around: 27 sc.

Stuff Leg with polyester fiberfill.

Rnds 18 and 19: (Sc in next sc, sc2tog) around: 12 sc.

Rnd 20: Sc2tog around; slip st in next sc, finish off and hide yarn end: 6 sc.

SOLE

With Contrasting Color, work same as Body, page 11, through Rnd 3: 18 sc.

Slip st in next sc, finish off leaving a long end for sewing.

Sew Sole to the bottom of Leg *(Photo 7)*; hide yarn ends.

Photo 7

ARM (Make 2)

Rnd 1 (Right side)**:** With Main Color, make an adjustable loop to form a ring; work 6 sc in ring; do **not** join, place marker.

Rnds 2-9: Sc in each sc around.

Slip st in next sc, finish off leaving a long end for sewing.

TAIL

Rnd 1 (Right side)**:** With Main Color, make an adjustable loop to form a ring; work 6 sc in ring; do **not** join, place marker.

Rnd 2: Sc in each sc around.

Rnd 3: (Sc in next sc, 2 sc in next sc) around: 9 sc.

Rnd 4: (Sc in next 2 sc, 2 sc in next sc) around: 12 sc.

Rnd 5: (Sc in next 3 sc, 2 sc in next sc) around: 15 sc.

Rnd 6: Sc in each sc around.

Rnd 7: (Sc in next 4 sc, 2 sc in next sc) around: 18 sc.

Rnd 8: (Sc in next 5 sc, 2 sc in next sc) around: 21 sc.

Rnd 9: (Sc in next 6 sc, 2 sc in next sc) around: 24 sc.

Rnd 10: Sc in each sc around.

Rnd 11: (Sc in next 7 sc, 2 sc in next sc) around: 27 sc.

Rnd 12: Sc in each sc around.

Rnd 13: (Sc in next 8 sc, 2 sc in next sc) around; slip st in next sc, finish off leaving a long end for sewing: 30 sc.

BODY ASSEMBLY

Sew Legs to the Body to be in a standing position. Insert the yarn ends through the Body and out the neck; do **not** cut yarn.

Flatten last rnd of Arms and sew closed. Sew Arms to Body on the third rnd from the top, placing them at a slight angle towards the front. Insert the yarn ends through the Body and out the neck; do **not** cut yarn.

Sew Tail to Body, beginning in the third rnd up from the bottom and stuffing with polyester fiberfill before closing. Insert the yarn ends through the Body and out the neck; do **not** cut yarn.

Tie all strands together at the neck, then hide all yarn ends in Body.

Sew Head to Body, sewing around the neck 3 times; secure and hide yarn end.

LAMB

Finished Size: Approximately 7" (18 cm) tall (seated)

SHOPPING LIST

YARN

(Medium Weight) MEDIUM 4

- ☐ Tan - 125 yards (114 meters)
- ☐ Brown - 22 yards (20 meters)

(Bulky Weight) BULKY 5

- ☐ White - 62 yards (56.5 meters)

CROCHET HOOKS

- ☐ Size E (3.5 mm) **and**
- ☐ Size 7 (4.5 mm)

ADDITIONAL SUPPLIES

- ☐ Safety pin - for optional marker
- ☐ Yarn needle
- ☐ Polyester fiberfill

GAUGE INFORMATION

Gauge for the lamb is **not** of great importance as long as your crochet fabric is very dense ***(see Gauge, page 43)***.

STITCH GUIDE

SINGLE CROCHET 2 TOGETHER
(abbreviated sc2tog)
Pull up a loop in each of next 2 sc, YO and draw through all 3 loops on hook **(counts as one sc)**.

HEAD

Rnd 1 (Right side)**:** With smaller size hook and Tan, make an adjustable loop to form a ring ***(Figs. 1a-d, page 44)***; work 6 sc in ring; do **not** join, place marker to indicate beginning of rnd ***(see Markers, page 45)***.

Rnd 2: 2 Sc in each sc around: 12 sc.

Rnd 3: (Sc in next sc, 2 sc in next sc) around: 18 sc.

Rnd 4: (Sc in next 2 sc, 2 sc in next sc) around: 24 sc.

Rnd 5: (Sc in next 3 sc, 2 sc in next sc) around: 30 sc.

Rnds 6-8: Sc in each sc around.

Rnd 9: (Sc in next 4 sc, 2 sc in next sc) around: 36 sc.

Rnds 10 and 11: Sc in each sc around.

Rnd 12: (Sc in next 4 sc, sc2tog) around: 30 sc.

Rnd 13: Sc in each sc around.

Rnd 14: Sc in each sc around changing to White bulky yarn in last sc *(Fig. 3a, page 45)*; cut Tan.

Change to larger size hook.

Rnd 15: (Sc in next 4 sc, 2 sc in next sc) around: 36 sc.

Rnd 16: (Sc in next 5 sc, 2 sc in next sc) around: 42 sc.

Rnds 17 and 18: Sc in each sc around.

Rnd 19: (Sc in next 5 sc, sc2tog) around: 36 sc.

Rnd 20: (Sc in next 4 sc, sc2tog) around: 30 sc.

Rnd 21: (Sc in next 3 sc, sc2tog) around: 24 sc.

Rnd 22: (Sc in next 2 sc, sc2tog) around: 18 sc.

Stuff Head with polyester fiberfill.

Rnd 23: (Sc in next sc, sc2tog) around: 12 sc.

Rnd 24: Sc2tog around; slip st in next sc, finish off leaving a long end for sewing: 6 sc.

Weave yarn end through the sts on the last rnd to close ***(Fig. 4, page 46)***; secure yarn, then insert it through the Head and out on Rnd 15 where it will be attached to the Body ***(Photo 1)***; do **not** cut yarn.

Photo 1

EAR (Make 2)

Work same as Head, page 14, through Rnd 3: 18 sc.

Rnds 4 and 5: Sc in each sc around.

Rnd 6 (Decrease rnd)**:** (Sc in next sc, sc2tog) around: 12 sc.

Rnds 7-9: Repeat Rnds 4-6: 8 sc.

Rnd 10: Sc in each sc around; slip st in next sc, finish off leaving a long end for sewing.

HEAD ASSEMBLY

Use photos as guides for placement of all pieces. See Tips, page 44, for important information on safety, stuffing, and yarn ends.

Use whipstitch ***(Figs. 5a & b, page 46)*** for the method of sewing to join the pieces together.

Flatten Ears and sew across the edge to close, then sew Ears to Rnd 20 of the Head. Insert the yarn ends through the Head and out near the other yarn end; do **not** cut yarn.

Tie all strands together at the neck, then hide the Ear yarn ends in Head.

With Brown, insert needle near the other yarn end and back out through the beginning ring. Embroider nose using straight stitch ***(Fig. 6, page 46)***, then embroider eyes on Rnd 12, 4 sts apart using satin stitch ***(Fig. 7b, page 46) (Photo 2)***.
Finish by pushing the needle back through the Head and out the bottom. Knot the two ends together, then hide the ends in Head.

Photo 2

BODY

Rnd 1 (Right side)**:** With larger size hook and White bulky yarn, make an adjustable loop to form a ring; work 6 sc in ring; do **not** join, place marker.

Rnd 2: 2 Sc in each sc around: 12 sc.

Rnd 3: (Sc in next sc, 2 sc in next sc) around: 18 sc.

Rnd 4: (Sc in next 2 sc, 2 sc in next sc) around: 24 sc.

Rnd 5: (Sc in next 3 sc, 2 sc in next sc) around: 30 sc.

Rnd 6: (Sc in next 4 sc, 2 sc in next sc) around: 36 sc.

Rnd 7: (Sc in next 5 sc, 2 sc in next sc) around: 42 sc.

Rnd 8: (Sc in next 6 sc, 2 sc in next sc) around: 48 sc.

Rnds 9-13: Sc in each sc around.

Rnd 14: (Sc in next 6 sc, sc2tog) around: 42 sc.

Rnd 15: (Sc in next 5 sc, sc2tog) around: 36 sc.

Rnd 16: (Sc in next 4 sc, sc2tog) around: 30 sc.

Rnds 17-19: Sc in each sc around.

Rnd 20: (Sc in next 3 sc, sc2tog) around: 24 sc.

Rnd 21: (Sc in next 2 sc, sc2tog) around: 18 sc.

Stuff Body with polyester fiberfill.

Rnd 22: (Sc in next sc, sc2tog) around: 12 sc.

Rnd 23: Sc2tog around; slip st in next sc, finish off leaving a long end: 6 sc.

LEG (Make 2)

Rnd 1 (Right side)**:** With smaller size hook and Brown, make an adjustable loop to form a ring; work 6 sc in ring; do **not** join, place marker.

Rnds 2-4: Work same as Body Rnds 2-4: 24 sc.

Rnd 5: Sc in each sc around changing to Tan in last sc; cut Brown.

Rnds 6 and 7: Sc in each sc around.

Rnd 8: (Sc in next 2 sc, sc2tog) around: 18 sc.

Rnd 9: Sc in each sc around.

Rnd 10: (Sc in next 4 sc, sc2tog) around: 15 sc.

Stuff Leg with polyester fiberfill as you work, lightly stuffing last 5 rnds.

Rnds 11-24: Sc in each sc around.

Slip st in next sc, finish off leaving a long end for sewing ***(Photo 3)***.

Photo 3

ARM (Make 2)

Work same as Leg.

TAIL

With larger size hook and White bulky yarn, ch 5.

Row 1: Sc in second ch from hook and in each ch across; finish off leaving a long end for sewing.

BODY ASSEMBLY

Flatten last rnd of Legs and sew closed. Sew Legs to Rnd 6 of the Body. Insert the yarn ends through the Body and out the neck; do **not** cut yarn.

Flatten last rnd of Arms and sew closed. Sew Arms across Rnds 17-19 of Body placing them at a slight angle. Insert the yarn ends through the Body and out the neck ***(Photo 4)***; do **not** cut yarn.

Photo 4

Sew Tail to Rnds 7 and 8 of Body ***(Photo 5)***. Insert the yarn ends through the Body and out the neck; do **not** cut yarn.

Photo 5

Tie all strands together at the neck, then hide all yarn ends in the Body.

Sew Head to Body, sewing around the neck 3 times; secure and hide yarn end.

DOLL

Finished Size: Approximately 9" (23 cm) tall

Blanket instructions on page 22.

SHOPPING LIST

YARN

(Light Weight) LIGHT 3

☐ Grey - 130 yards (119 meters)

(Medium Weight) MEDIUM 4

☐ Skin color - 60 yards (55 meters)

☐ Pink - 6 yards (5.5 meters)

CROCHET HOOK

☐ Size E (3.5 mm)

ADDITIONAL SUPPLIES

☐ Safety pin - for optional marker

☐ Brown embroidery floss

☐ Pink embroidery floss

☐ Yarn and tapestry needles

☐ Polyester fiberfill

GAUGE INFORMATION

Gauge for the doll is **not** of great importance as long as your crochet fabric is very dense ***(see Gauge, page 43)***.

STITCH GUIDE

SINGLE CROCHET 2 TOGETHER

(abbreviated sc2tog)

Pull up a loop in each of next 2 sc, YO and draw through all 3 loops on hook **(counts as one sc)**.

HEAD

Rnd 1 (Right side)**:** With Skin color, make an adjustable loop to form a ring ***(Figs. 1a-d, page 44)***; work 6 sc in ring; do **not** join, place marker to indicate beginning of rnd ***(see Markers, page 45)***.

Rnd 2: 2 Sc in each sc around: 12 sc.

Rnd 3: (Sc in next sc, 2 sc in next sc) around: 18 sc.

Rnd 4: (Sc in next 2 sc, 2 sc in next sc) around: 24 sc.

Rnd 5: (Sc in next 3 sc, 2 sc in next sc) around: 30 sc.

Rnd 6: (Sc in next 4 sc, 2 sc in next sc) around: 36 sc.

Rnd 7: (Sc in next 5 sc, 2 sc in next sc) around: 42 sc.

Rnd 8: (Sc in next 6 sc, 2 sc in next sc) around: 48 sc.

Rnd 9: (Sc in next 7 sc, 2 sc in next sc) around: 54 sc.

Rnds 10-15: Sc in each sc around.

Rnd 16: (Sc in next 7 sc, sc2tog) around: 48 sc.

Rnd 17: (Sc in next 6 sc, sc2tog) around: 42 sc.

Rnd 18: (Sc in next 5 sc, sc2tog) around: 36 sc.

Rnd 19: (Sc in next 4 sc, sc2tog) around: 30 sc.

Rnd 20: (Sc in next 3 sc, sc2tog) around: 24 sc.

Rnd 21: (Sc in next 2 sc, sc2tog) around: 18 sc.

Stuff Head with polyester fiberfill.

Rnd 22: (Sc in next sc, sc2tog) around: 12 sc.

Rnd 23: Sc2tog around; slip st in next sc, finish off leaving a long end for sewing: 6 sc.

HAT

Rnd 1 (Right side)**:** With Grey, make an adjustable loop to form a ring; work 6 sc in ring; do **not** join, place marker.

Rnd 2: 2 Sc in each sc around: 12 sc.

Rnd 3: (Hdc in next sc, 2 hdc in next sc) around: 18 hdc.

Rnd 4: (Hdc in next 2 hdc, 2 hdc in next hdc) around: 24 hdc.

Rnd 5: (Hdc in next 3 hdc, 2 hdc in next hdc) around: 30 hdc.

Rnd 6: (Hdc in next 4 hdc, 2 hdc in next hdc) around: 36 hdc.

Rnd 7: (Hdc in next 5 hdc, 2 hdc in next hdc) around: 42 hdc.

Rnds 8-10: Hdc in each hdc around.

Rnd 11: Hdc in each hdc around changing to Pink in last hdc *(Fig. 3b, page 45)*; cut Grey.

Rnd 12: Sc in each hdc around; slip st in next sc, finish off leaving a long end for sewing.

HEAD ASSEMBLY

Use photos as guides for placement of all pieces. See Tips, page 44, for important information on safety, stuffing, and yarn ends.

Use whipstitch *(Figs. 5a & b, page 46)* for the method of sewing to join the pieces together.

Sew the Hat to the Head, placing it at an angle *(Photo 1)*.

Photo 1

Insert the yarn ends through the Head and out the beginning ring where it will be attached to the Body; do **not** cut yarn.

With Pink embroidery floss, insert needle in at the bottom of the Head and back out on Rnd 7. Embroider mouth using satin stitch *(Fig. 7b, page 46)*.
Finish by pushing the needle back through the Head and out near the other yarn end. Knot the two ends together, then hide the ends.

With Skin color, embroider nose on Rnds 9 and 10 in same manner.

With Brown embroidery floss, embroider eyes on Rnd 11, 7 sc apart in same manner.

FIRST LEG

Rnd 1 (Right side)**:** With Grey, make an adjustable loop to form a ring; work 6 sc in ring; do **not** join, place marker.

Rnd 2: 2 Sc in each sc around: 12 sc.

Rnd 3: (Sc in next sc, 2 sc in next sc) around: 18 sc.

Rnd 4: (Sc in next 2 sc, 2 sc in next sc) around: 24 sc.

Rnd 5: Sc in next 14 sc, sc2tog, (sc in next 2 sc, sc2tog) twice: 21 sc.

Rnd 6: Sc in next 15 sc, sc2tog 3 times: 18 sc.

Rnd 7: Sc in next 14 sc, sc2tog twice: 16 sc.

Rnds 8-13: Sc in each sc around.

Rnd 14: Sc in next 6 sc, sc2tog twice, sc in next 6 sc: 14 sc.

Rnd 15: Sc in each sc around.

Rnd 16: (2 Sc in next sc, sc in next 6 sc) twice: 16 sc.

Rnds 17-19: Sc in each sc around.

Slip st in next sc, finish off leaving a long end for sewing.

SECOND LEG

Work same as First Leg through Rnd 18: 16 sc.

Joining: Sc in next 6 sc, working in next sc **and** in same sc as slip st on First Leg, sc2tog, sc in next 7 sc; remove marker and place marker here to indicate the new beginning of rnd *(Photo 2)*; do **not** finish off.

BODY

Rnd 1: Sc in next 7 sc, working in last sc on same Leg and in next sc on next Leg, sc2tog, sc in each sc around: 30 sc.

Rnd 2: (Sc in next 3 sc, 2 sc in next sc) 3 times, sc in each sc around: 33 sc.

Rnd 3: (Sc in next 4 sc, 2 sc in next sc) 3 times, sc in each sc around: 36 sc.

Rnds 4-6: Sc in each sc around.

Rnd 7: (Sc in next 4 sc, sc2tog) 3 times, sc in each sc around: 33 sc.

Rnd 8: Sc in next 6 sc, sc2tog, (sc in next sc, sc2tog) twice, sc in each sc around: 30 sc.

Rnds 9-13: Sc in each sc around.

Stuff Legs and Body with polyester fiberfill as you work.

Rnd 14: (Sc in next 3 sc, sc2tog) around: 24 sc.

Rnds 15 and 16: Sc in each sc around.

Rnd 17: (Sc in next 2 sc, sc2tog) around: 18 sc.

Rnds 18-20: Sc in each sc around.

Rnd 21: Sc2tog around: 9 sc.

Continue to decrease around until hole is closed; slip st in next sc, finish off leaving a long end ***(Photo 3)***.

ARM (Make 2)

Rnd 1 (Right side)**:** With Skin color, make an adjustable loop to form a ring; work 6 sc in ring; do **not** join, place marker.

Rnd 2: 2 Sc in each sc around: 12 sc.

Rnd 3: (Sc in next sc, 2 sc in next sc) around: 18 sc.

Rnd 4: (Sc in next 4 sc, sc2tog) around: 15 sc.

Rnd 5: (Sc in next 3 sc, sc2tog) around changing to Pink in last sc ***(Fig. 3a, page 45)***; cut Skin color: 12 sc.

Rnd 6: Sc in each sc around changing to Grey in last sc; cut Pink.

Rnd 7: (Sc in next sc, 2 sc in next sc) around: 18 sc.

Stuff Arm with polyester fiberfill as you work.

Rnds 8-13: Sc in each sc around.

Rnd 14: (Sc in next 4 sc, sc2tog) around: 15 sc.

Rnds 15 and 16: Sc in each sc around.

Rnd 17: (Sc in next 3 sc, sc2tog) around: 12 sc.

Rnds 18 and 19: Sc in each sc around.

Slip st in next sc, finish off leaving a long end for sewing.

BODY ASSEMBLY

Flatten last rnd of Arms and sew closed. Sew Arms to Body on the third rnd from the top. Insert the yarn ends through the Body and out the neck; do **not** cut yarn.

Tie all strands together at the neck, then hide all yarn ends in the Body.

Sew Head to Body, sewing around the neck 3 times; secure and hide yarn end.

BLANKET

The Blanket can be made in colors to match any of the toys.

SIZE INFORMATION

Car Seat Blanket: 29" x 35" (73.5 cm x 89 cm)

Doll Blanket: 12" (30.5 cm) square

Size Note: We have printed the instructions for the sizes in different colors to make it easier for you to find:

- Car Seat Blanket in Blue
- Doll Blanket in Pink

Instructions in Black apply to both sizes.

SHOPPING LIST

YARN

(Medium Weight) MEDIUM 4

[6 ounces, 315 yards (170.1 grams, 288 meters) per skein]:

- ☐ Color A (Pink) - 1 skein
- ☐ Color B (Grey) - 1 skein
- ☐ Color C (White) - 1 skein

Note: Light weight yarn can be used when needed to match the color of the toy as long as gauge can be achieved.

CROCHET HOOK

- ☐ Size 7 (4.5 mm)
  or size needed for gauge

ADDITIONAL SUPPLIES

- ☐ Yarn needle

GAUGE INFORMATION

In pattern, 10 sts = 3" (7.5 cm)

Gauge Swatch: 3" (7.5 cm) wide

With Color A, ch 11.

Row 1: Hdc in second ch from hook and in each ch across: 10 hdc.

Rows 2-6: Ch 1, turn; hdc in each hdc across.

Finish off.

STITCH GUIDE

BEGINNING LINKED DOUBLE CROCHET
(abbreviated beginning linked dc)

Insert hook in second ch from hook, YO and pull up a loop, insert hook in first hdc, YO and pull up a loop (3 loops on hook), (YO and draw through 2 loops on hook) twice.

LINKED DOUBLE CROCHET ***(abbreviated linked dc)***

Insert hook in horizontal bar of previous linked dc ***(Fig. A)***, YO and pull up a loop, insert hook in next st, YO and pull up a loop (3 loops on hook) ***(Fig. B)***, (YO and draw through 2 loops on hook) twice ***(Fig. C)***.

EASY

Fig. A

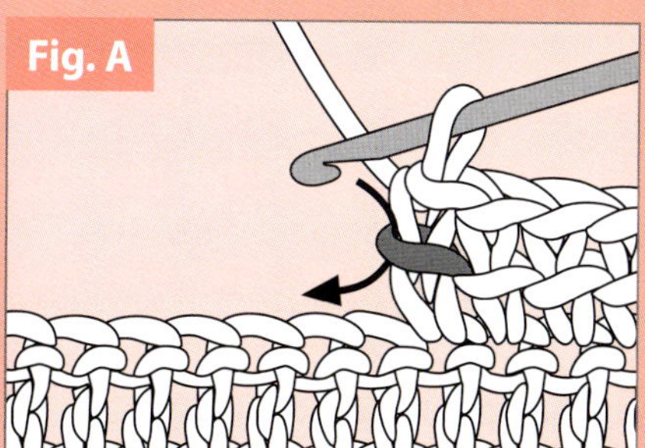

Fig. B

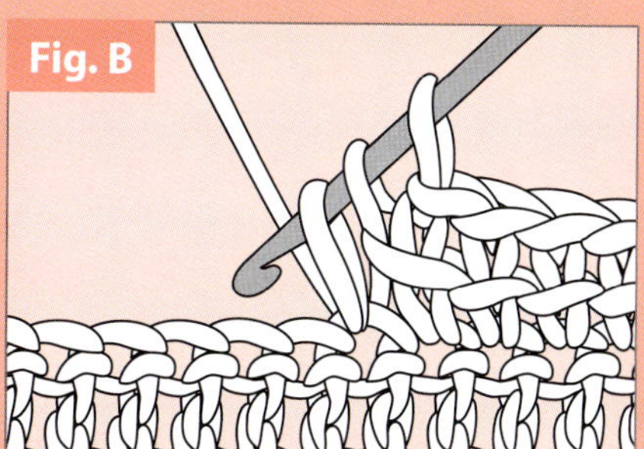

Fig. C

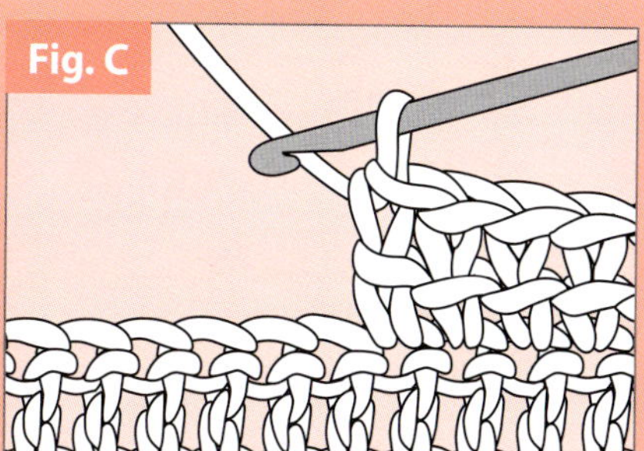

BODY

With Color B, ch 96{39}.

Row 1 (Right side)**:** Hdc in second ch from hook and in each ch across changing to Color C in last hdc ***(Fig. 3b, page 45)***: 95{38} hdc.

Row 2: Ch 1, turn; hdc in each hdc across changing to Color A in last hdc.

Row 3: Ch 2 (does **not** count as a st), turn; dc in each hdc across changing to Color B in last dc ***(Fig. 3c, page 45)***.

Row 4: Ch 1, turn; hdc in each dc across changing to Color C in last hdc.

Repeat Rows 2-4 for pattern until Body measures approximately 34½{11½}"/87.5{29} cm from beginning ch, ending by working Row 2.

EDGING

With Color A, ch 2, turn; work beginning linked dc, work linked dc around entire edge, working 4 linked dc in each corner; join with slip st to first st, finish off.

TURTLE

●●○○ EASY +

Finished Size: Approximately 6" (15 cm) tall

SHOPPING LIST

YARN

(Medium Weight) MEDIUM 4

Turtle

- ☐ Light Green - 135 yards (123 meters)
- ☐ Dark Green - 36 yards (33 meters)
- ☐ Green - 16 yards (14.5 meters)

Strawberry

- ☐ Red - 16 yards (14.5 meters)
- ☐ Green - 5 yards (4.5 meters)

CROCHET HOOK

- ☐ Size E (3.5 mm)

ADDITIONAL SUPPLIES

- ☐ Safety pin - for optional marker
- ☐ Black embroidery floss
- ☐ Yarn and tapestry needles
- ☐ Polyester fiberfill
- ☐ 10.5 mm safety eyes - 2 (Please take caution if the toy is for a child that is at risk of choking. See Safety, page 44.)

GAUGE INFORMATION

Gauge for the turtle and strawberry are **not** of great importance as long as your crochet fabric is very dense *(see Gauge, page 43)*.

STITCH GUIDE

SINGLE CROCHET 2 TOGETHER

(abbreviated sc2tog)

Pull up a loop in each of next 2 sc, YO and draw through all 3 loops on hook **(counts as one sc)**.

HEAD

Rnd 1 (Right side)**:** With Light Green, make an adjustable loop to form a ring ***(Figs. 1a-d, page 44)***; work 6 sc in ring; do **not** join, place marker to indicate beginning of rnd ***(see Markers, page 45)***.

Rnd 2: 2 Sc in each sc around: 12 sc.

Rnd 3: (Sc in next sc, 2 sc in next sc) around: 18 sc.

Rnd 4: (Sc in next 2 sc, 2 sc in next sc) around: 24 sc.

Rnd 5: (Sc in next 3 sc, 2 sc in next sc) around: 30 sc.

Rnd 6: (Sc in next 4 sc, 2 sc in next sc) around: 36 sc.

Rnd 7: (Sc in next 5 sc, 2 sc in next sc) around: 42 sc.

Rnd 8: (Sc in next 6 sc, 2 sc in next sc) around: 48 sc.

Rnds 9 and 10: Sc in each sc around.

Rnd 11: (Sc in next 6 sc, sc2tog) around: 42 sc.

Rnds 12 and 13: Sc in each sc around.

Use photos as guides for placement of all pieces. See Tips, page 44, for important information on safety, stuffing, and yarn ends.

Attach safety eyes to Rnd 11 of Head spacing the posts approximately 8 sts apart one st out from a decrease *(Photo 1)*.

Rnd 14: (Sc in next 5 sc, sc2tog) around: 36 sc.

Rnds 15 and 16: Sc in each sc around.

Rnd 17: (Sc in next 4 sc, sc2tog) around: 30 sc.

Rnd 18: (Sc in next 3 sc, sc2tog) around: 24 sc.

Rnds 19 and 20: Sc in each sc around.

Stuff Head with polyester fiberfill.

Rnd 21: (Sc in next 2 sc, sc2tog) around: 18 sc.

Rnds 22-33: Sc in each sc around.

Slip st in next sc, finish off leaving a long end for sewing.

HEAD ASSEMBLY

Use whipstitch *(Figs. 5a & b, page 46)* for the method of sewing to join the pieces together.

Complete stuffing the Head with polyester fiberfill, leaving the neck soft.

Pinch the area between the eyes together to form a bridge. Using a long end, make a couple of sts from side to side near the inner edge of the safety eyes to hold it in place; secure yarn.

Insert the needle through the Head and out 4 rnds below to the mouth area *(Photo 2)*. Embroider the mouth across 5 stitches using straight stitch *(Fig. 6, page 46)*, stitching tightly to cause a dent.

Insert the yarn ends through the Head and out where it will be attached to the Body; do **not** cut yarn.

Photo 2

BELLY

Work same as Head, page 25, through Rnd 8: 48 sc.

Rnd 9: (Sc in next 7 sc, 2 sc in next sc) around: 54 sc.

Rnd 10: (Sc in next 8 sc, 2 sc in next sc) around: 60 sc.

Rnd 11: Sc in each sc around; slip st in next sc, finish off leaving a long end for sewing.

LEG (Make 4)

Work same as Head, page 25, through Rnd 4: 24 sc.

Rnds 5 and 6: Sc in each sc around.

Rnd 7: (Sc in next 2 sc, sc2tog) around: 18 sc.

Rnd 8: (Sc in next sc, sc2tog) around: 12 sc.

Rnds 9-13: Sc in each sc around.

Slip st in next sc, finish off leaving a long end for sewing.

Stuff Legs leaving the last 3 rnds unstuffed.

TAIL

Rnd 1 (Right side)**:** With Light Green, make an adjustable loop to form a ring; work 6 sc in ring; do **not** join, place marker.

Rnds 2-4: Sc in each sc around.

Slip st in next sc, finish off leaving a long end for sewing.

SHELL

HEXAGON (Make 7)

Rnd 1 (Right side)**:** With Green, make an adjustable loop to form a ring; work 6 sc in ring; do **not** join, place marker.

Rnd 2: 2 Sc in each sc around: 12 sc.

Rnd 3: (Sc in next sc, 2 sc in next sc) around changing to Dark Green in last sc *(Fig. 3a, page 45)*; cut Green: 18 sc.

Rnd 4: (Sc in next 2 sc, 2 sc in next sc) around; slip st in next sc, finish off leaving a long end for sewing: 24 sc.

JOINING

Sew two Hexagons together across 4 sts, beginning in second sc of 2-sc group and ending in first sc of next 2-sc group ***(Photo 3)***; do **not** cut yarn.

Photo 3

Continuing around the Hexagon that will be in the center, sew the remaining Hexagons in place in same manner. Sew sides of Hexagons together. Tie all strands together at the center; cut ends short ***(Photo 4)***.

Photo 4

EDGING

Rnd 1: With **right** side facing and working around edge of Shell, join Dark Green with sc in any seam ***(see Joining With Sc, page 45)***; sc in next 12 sc, (sc in next seam, sc in next 12 sc) around; do **not** join, place marker: 78 sc.

Rnd 2: (Sc2tog, sc in next 11 sc) around: 72 sc.

Rnd 3: Sc in each sc around.

Rnd 4: (Sc2tog, sc in next 10 sc) around: 66 sc.

Rnds 5-7: Sc in each sc around.

Rnd 8: (Sc2tog, sc in next 9 sc) around; slip st in next sc, finish off leaving a long end for sewing ***(Photo 5)***: 60 sc.

Photo 5

BODY ASSEMBLY

Arrange the Head, Legs, and Tail evenly around the Belly. Flatten last rnd of all pieces with long ends at side ***(Photo 6)***.

Photo 6

Sew one piece to each of the six straight edges of the Belly, working through both loops of all 3 layers.

Tie all strands together at the center of the Belly *(Photo 7)*; cut ends short.

Beginning at the Head, sew the Shell to the Belly, stuffing piece with polyester fiberfill before closing; secure yarn. Sew the back of the Head to the Shell so the neck and Head stay upright *(Photo 8)*; secure and hide yarn end.

STRAWBERRY

Rnd 1 (Right side)**:** With Red, make an adjustable loop to form a ring; work 6 sc in ring; do **not** join, place marker.

Rnd 2: 2 Sc in each sc around: 12 sc.

Rnd 3: (Sc in next sc, 2 sc in next sc) around: 18 sc.

Rnds 4 and 5: Sc in each sc around.

Rnd 6: (Sc in next sc, 2 sc in next sc) around: 27 sc.

Rnd 7: Sc in next sc, (2 sc in next sc, sc in next sc) around: 40 sc.

Rnd 8: Sc in each sc around.

Rnd 9: Sc in next sc, (sc2tog, sc in next sc) around: 27 sc.

Rnd 10: Sc in next sc, sc2tog around: 14 sc.

Stuff Strawberry with polyester fiberfill.

Rnd 11: Sc2tog around; slip st in next sc, finish off leaving a long end for sewing: 7 sc.

Weave yarn end through the sts on the last rnd *(Fig. 4, page 46)*; secure and hide yarn end.

LEAVES

Rnd 1 (Right side)**:** With Green, (ch 5, sc in fifth ch from hook) 4 times; join with slip st in ch at base of first sc.

Rnd 2: (Sc in next 4 chs, skip next sc) around; join with slip st to first sc, finish off leaving a long end for sewing.

Sew Leaves to the top of Strawberry; secure and hide yarn end.

With Black embroidery floss, embroider seeds around the Strawberry using straight stitch *(Fig. 6, page 46)*.

TEDDY BEAR

Finished Size: Approximately 4½" (11.5 cm) tall (seated)

SHOPPING LIST

YARN

(Light Weight) LIGHT 3
- ☐ Grey - 95 yards (87 meters)

(Medium Weight) MEDIUM 4
- ☐ White - 8 yards (7.5 meters)
- ☐ Pink - 6 yards (5.5 meters)

CROCHET HOOK

- ☐ Size E (3.5 mm) for Bear
- ☐ Size H (5 mm) for Scarf

ADDITIONAL SUPPLIES

- ☐ Safety pin - for optional marker
- ☐ White felt - small piece
- ☐ Black embroidery floss
- ☐ White embroidery floss
- ☐ Sewing needle
- ☐ Yarn and tapestry needles
- ☐ Polyester fiberfill

GAUGE INFORMATION

Gauge for the bear is **not** of great importance as long as your crochet fabric is very dense *(see Gauge, page 43)*.

STITCH GUIDE

SINGLE CROCHET 2 TOGETHER
(abbreviated sc2tog)
Pull up a loop in each of next 2 sc, YO and draw through all 3 loops on hook **(counts as one sc)**.

HEAD

Rnd 1 (Right side)**:** With Grey, make an adjustable loop to form a ring ***(Figs. 1a-d, page 44)***; work 6 sc in ring; do **not** join, place marker to indicate beginning of rnd ***(see Markers, page 45)***.

Rnd 2: 2 Sc in each sc around: 12 sc.

Rnd 3: (Sc in next sc, 2 sc in next sc) around: 18 sc.

Rnd 4: (Sc in next 2 sc, 2 sc in next sc) around: 24 sc.

Rnd 5: (Sc in next 3 sc, 2 sc in next sc) around: 30 sc.

Rnd 6: (Sc in next 4 sc, 2 sc in next sc) around: 36 sc.

Rnd 7: (Sc in next 5 sc, 2 sc in next sc) around: 42 sc.

Rnd 8: (Sc in next 6 sc, 2 sc in next sc) around: 48 sc.

Rnds 9-11: Sc in each sc around.

Rnd 12: (Sc in next 6 sc, sc2tog) around: 42 sc.

Rnd 13: (Sc in next 5 sc, sc2tog) around: 36 sc.

Rnd 14: (Sc in next 4 sc, sc2tog) around: 30 sc.

Rnd 15: (Sc in next 3 sc, sc2tog) around: 24 sc.

Rnd 16: (Sc in next 2 sc, sc2tog) around: 18 sc.

Stuff Head with polyester fiberfill.

Rnd 17: (Sc in next sc, sc2tog) around: 12 sc.

Rnd 18: Sc2tog around; slip st in next sc, finish off leaving a long end for sewing: 6 sc.

EAR (Make 2)

Work same as Head through Rnd 4: 24 sc.

Slip st in next sc, finish off leaving a long end for sewing.

MUZZLE

With White, work same as Head through Rnd 3: 18 sc.

Rnd 4: (Sc in next 8 sc, 2 sc in next sc) twice; slip st in next sc, finish off leaving a long end for sewing: 20 sc.

HEAD ASSEMBLY

Use photos as guides for placement of all pieces. See Tips, page 44, for important information on safety, stuffing, and yarn ends.

Use whipstitch *(Figs. 5a & b, page 46)* for the method of sewing to join the pieces together.

Flatten Ears and sew across the edge to close; do **not** cut yarn.

Using the Ears as guides, cut 2 pieces of felt slightly smaller than the Ears.

Using white embroidery floss and sewing needle, sew felt pieces in place *(Photo 1)*.

Photo 1

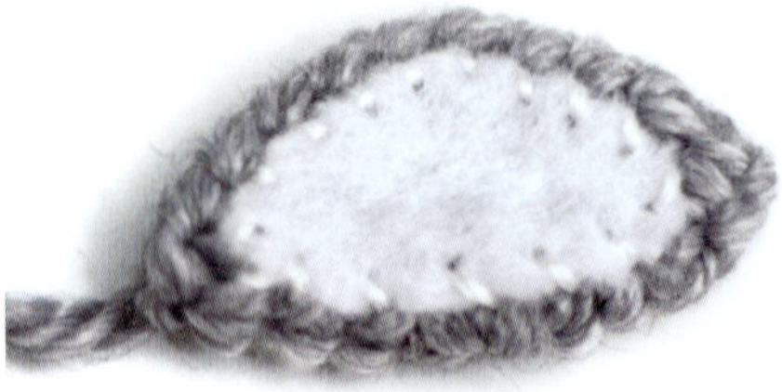

Using long yarn ends and yarn needle, sew folded edge of Ears diagonally down the side of the Head across Rnds 3-10. Insert the yarn ends through the Head and out near the other yarn end where it will be attached to the Body; do **not** cut yarn.

Sew Muzzle to Head, beginning on Rnd 10 and ending three rounds up from the base. Insert the yarn ends through the Head and out near the other yarn ends *(Photo 2)*; do **not** cut yarn.

Photo 2

Tie all strands together at the neck, then hide Ear and Muzzle yarn ends in Head.

With Black embroidery floss, insert needle at the bottom of the Head and back out on Rnd 1 of the Muzzle. Embroider nose using satin stitch and forming a triangle *(Figs. 7a & b, page 46)*. Embroider eyes on Rnd 9, 5 sts apart using satin stitch.
Finish by pushing the needle back through the Head and out near the other floss end *(Photo 3)*. Knot the two ends together, then hide the ends.

Photo 3

BODY

Rnd 1 (Right side)**:** With Grey, make an adjustable loop to form a ring; work 6 sc in ring; do **not** join, place marker.

Rnd 2: 2 Sc in each sc around: 12 sc.

Rnd 3: (Sc in next sc, 2 sc in next sc) around: 18 sc.

Rnd 4: (Sc in next 2 sc, 2 sc in next sc) around: 24 sc.

Rnd 5: (Sc in next 3 sc, 2 sc in next sc) around: 30 sc.

Rnds 6-9: Sc in each sc around.

Rnd 10: (Sc in next 4 sc, 2 sc in next sc) around: 36 sc.

Rnds 11-14: Sc in each sc around.

Rnd 15: (Sc in next 4 sc, sc2tog) around: 30 sc.

Rnd 16: (Sc in next 3 sc, sc2tog) around: 24 sc.

Rnd 17: (Sc in next 2 sc, sc2tog) around: 18 sc.

Stuff Body with polyester fiberfill.

Rnd 18: (Sc in next sc, sc2tog) around: 12 sc.

Rnd 19: Sc2tog around; slip st in next sc, finish off leaving a long end: 6 sc.

Weave yarn end through the sts on the last rnd ***(Fig. 4, page 46)***; secure yarn, then insert it through the Body and out the beginning ring where it will be attached to the Head ***(Photo 4)***; do **not** cut yarn.

Photo 4

LEG (Make 2)

Work same as Body through Rnd 4: 24 sc.

Rnd 5: Sc in each sc around.

Rnd 6: Sc in next 14 sc, sc2tog, (sc in next 2 sc, sc2tog) twice: 21 sc.

Rnd 7: Sc in next 13 sc, sc2tog 4 times: 17 sc.

Rnd 8: Sc in each sc around.

Rnd 9: Sc in next 13 sc, sc2tog twice: 15 sc.

Stuff Leg with polyester fiberfill.

Rnd 10: (Sc in next 3 sc, sc2tog) around: 12 sc.

Rnd 11: Sc in each sc around; slip st in next sc, finish off leaving a long end for sewing.

SOLE

With White, work same as Body through Rnd 3: 18 sc.

Slip st in next sc, finish off leaving a long end for sewing.

Sew Sole to the bottom of Leg ***(Photo 5)***; hide yarn ends.

Photo 5

ARM (Make 2)

Work same as Body through Rnd 3: 18 sc.

Rnd 4: Sc in each sc around.

Rnd 5: (Sc in next sc, sc2tog) around: 12 sc.

Rnd 6: Sc in each sc around.

Rnd 7: (Sc in next 2 sc, sc2tog) around: 9 sc.

Stuff Arm with polyester fiberfill.

Rnds 8-10: Sc in each sc around.

Slip st in next sc, finish off leaving a long end for sewing ***(Photo 6)***.

Photo 6

TAIL

Rnd 1 (Right side)**:** With Grey, make an adjustable loop to form a ring; work 6 sc in ring; do **not** join, place marker.

Rnd 2: 2 Sc in each sc around: 12 sc.

Rnd 3: Sc in each sc around; slip st in next sc, finish off leaving a long end for sewing.

BODY ASSEMBLY

Sew Legs to the Body to be in either a standing or sitting position with the shaping pointing forward. Insert the yarn ends through the Body and out the neck; do **not** cut yarn.

Leaving last 3 rnds of Arms unstuffed, flatten last rnd and sew closed. Sew Arms to Body on the fourth rnd from the top, placing them at a slight angle towards the front. Insert the yarn ends through the Body and out the neck; do **not** cut yarn.

Flatten the Tail and sew across the edge to close ***(Photo 7)***; do **not** cut yarn.

Photo 7

Sew Tail to Body, across 5 rnds, placed to help your Bear sit up straight if positioned to sit ***(Photos 8 & 9)***. Insert the yarn ends through the Body and out the neck; do **not** cut yarn.

Photo 8

Photo 9

Tie all strands together at the neck ***(Photo 10)***, then hide all yarn ends in the Body.

Photo 10

Sew Head to Body, sewing around the edge 3 times; secure and hide yarn end.

SCARF

With Pink and larger size hook, ch 31.

Row 1: Sc in second ch from hook and in each ch across: 30 sc.

Rows 2 and 3: Ch 1, turn; sc in each sc across.

Finish off and weave in ends.

Tie Scarf around Bear's neck and sew in place.

DUMBBELL RATTLE

BEGINNER

Finished Size: Approximately 5½" (14 cm) long

SHOPPING LIST

YARN

(Light Weight) LIGHT 3

- ☐ 115 yards (105 meters)

CROCHET HOOK

- ☐ Size E (3.5 mm)

ADDITIONAL SUPPLIES

- ☐ Safety pin - for optional marker
- ☐ Yarn needle
- ☐ Polyester fiberfill
- ☐ Rattle inserts (optional) - 2

GAUGE INFORMATION

Gauge for the rattle is **not** of great importance as long as your crochet fabric is very dense ***(see Gauge, page 43)***.

STITCH GUIDE

SINGLE CROCHET 2 TOGETHER

(abbreviated sc2tog)

Pull up a loop in each of next 2 sc, YO and draw through all 3 loops on hook **(counts as one sc)**.

END (Make 2)

Rnd 1 (Right side)**:** Make an adjustable loop to form a ring ***(Figs. 1a-d, page 44)***; work 6 sc in ring; do **not** join, place marker to indicate beginning of rnd ***(see Markers, page 45)***.

Rnd 2: 2 Sc in each sc around: 12 sc.

Rnd 3: (Sc in next sc, 2 sc in next sc) around: 18 sc.

Rnd 4: (Sc in next 2 sc, 2 sc in next sc) around: 24 sc.

Rnd 5: (Sc in next 3 sc, 2 sc in next sc) around: 30 sc.

Rnd 6: (Sc in next 4 sc, 2 sc in next sc) around: 36 sc.

Rnd 7: (Sc in next 5 sc, 2 sc in next sc) around: 42 sc.

Rnd 8: (Sc in next 6 sc, 2 sc in next sc) around: 48 sc.

Rnd 9: (Sc in next 7 sc, 2 sc in next sc) around: 54 sc.

Rnd 10: Sc in Back Loop Only of each sc around ***(Fig. 2, page 45)***.

Rnds 11 and 12: Sc in both loops of each sc around.

Rnd 13: (Sc in next 7 sc, sc2tog) around: 48 sc.

Rnds 14-16: Sc in each sc around.

Rnd 17: Working in Back Loops Only, (sc in next 6 sc, sc2tog) around: 42 sc.

Rnd 18: Working in both loops, (sc in next 5 sc, sc2tog) around: 36 sc.

Rnd 19: (Sc in next 4 sc, sc2tog) around: 30 sc.

Rnd 20: (Sc in next 3 sc, sc2tog) around: 24 sc.

See Tips, page 44, for important information on stuffing and yarn ends.

With bottom flat (Rnds 1-9), stuff End with polyester fiberfill, inserting rattle if desired ***(Photo 1)***.

Photo 1

Rnd 21: (Sc in next 2 sc, sc2tog) around: 18 sc.

Rnd 22: (Sc in next sc, sc2tog) around: 12 sc.

Rnd 23: Sc2tog around; slip st in next sc, finish off leaving a long end for sewing: 6 sc.

Press the beginning and ending rnds together to make piece look like a disk. Sew through the sides in 5 or 6 places to hold the shape ***(Photo 2)***; secure and hide yarn.

Photo 2

HANDLE

Rnd 1 (Right side)**:** Leaving a long end for sewing, make an adjustable loop to form a ring; work 6 sc in ring; do **not** join, place marker.

Rnd 2: 2 Sc in each sc around: 12 sc.

Rnd 3: Sc in each sc around.

Repeat Rnd 3 until Handle measures approximately 3" (7.5 cm).

Stuff Handle firmly with polyester fiberfill.

Last Rnd: Sc2tog around; slip st in next sc, finish off leaving a long end for sewing: 6 sc.

Using photo as a guide, whipstitch one end of Handle to Rnd 22 of one End ***(Fig. 5b, page 46)***, working around the edge twice.

Repeat with second End.

BUNNY

Finished Size: Approximately 7½" (19 cm) tall (standing)

SHOPPING LIST

YARN

(Medium Weight) 

Bunny

- ☐ Tan - 110 yards (101 meters)
- ☐ White - small amount

Carrot (each)

- ☐ Orange - 6 yards (5.5 meters)
- ☐ Green - small amount

CROCHET HOOK

- ☐ Size E (3.5 mm)

ADDITIONAL SUPPLIES

- ☐ Safety pin - for optional marker
- ☐ White embroidery floss
- ☐ Black embroidery floss
- ☐ Yarn and tapestry needles
- ☐ Polyester fiberfill
- ☐ Wire brush (to fluff tail)

GAUGE INFORMATION

Gauge for the bunny and carrot is **not** of great importance as long as your crochet fabric is very dense ***(see Gauge, page 43)***.

STITCH GUIDE

SINGLE CROCHET 2 TOGETHER

(abbreviated sc2tog)

Pull up a loop in each of next 2 sc, YO and draw through all 3 loops on hook **(counts as one sc)**.

HEAD

Rnd 1 (Right side)**:** With Tan, make an adjustable loop to form a ring ***(Figs. 1a-d, page 44)***; work 6 sc in ring; do **not** join, place marker to indicate beginning of rnd ***(see Markers, page 45)***.

Rnd 2: 2 Sc in each sc around: 12 sc.

Rnd 3: (Sc in next sc, 2 sc in next sc) around: 18 sc.

Rnd 4: (Sc in next 2 sc, 2 sc in next sc) around: 24 sc.

Rnd 5: (Sc in next 3 sc, 2 sc in next sc) around: 30 sc.

Rnd 6: (Sc in next 4 sc, 2 sc in next sc) around: 36 sc.

Rnd 7: (Sc in next 5 sc, 2 sc in next sc) around: 42 sc.

Rnds 8 and 9: Sc in each sc around.

Rnd 10: (Sc in next 5 sc, sc2tog) around: 36 sc.

Rnd 11: (Sc in next 4 sc, sc2tog) around: 30 sc.

Rnd 12: (Sc in next 3 sc, sc2tog) around: 24 sc.

Rnd 13: (Sc in next 2 sc, sc2tog) around: 18 sc.

Stuff Head with polyester fiberfill.

Rnd 14: (Sc in next sc, sc2tog) around: 12 sc.

Rnd 15: Sc2tog around; slip st in next sc, finish off leaving a long end for sewing: 6 sc.

EAR (Make 2)

Work same as Head through Rnd 4: 24 sc.

Rnds 5-12: Sc in each sc around.

Rnd 13: (Sc in next 2 sc, sc2tog) around: 18 sc.

Rnd 14: (Sc in next sc, sc2tog) around; slip st in next sc, finish off leaving a long end for sewing: 12 sc.

HEAD ASSEMBLY

Use photos as guides for placement of all pieces. See Tips, page 44, for important information on safety, stuffing, and yarn ends.

Use whipstitch ***(Figs. 5a & b, page 46)*** for the method of sewing to join the pieces together.

Flatten Ears and fold the bottom edge in half ***(Photo 1)***. Sew across the bottom edge to close, then sew Ears to Rnd 5 of the Head ***(Photo 2)***. Insert the yarn ends through the Head and out near the other yarn end where it will be attached to the Body; do **not** cut yarn.

Photo 1

Photo 2

Tie all strands together at the neck, then hide all but one yarn end in Head.

With White embroidery floss, insert the needle at the bottom of the Head and back out on Rnd 10, centered between the Ears. Embroider nose using satin stitch and forming a triangle ***(Figs. 7a & b, page 46)***. Finish by pushing the needle back through the Head and out near the other floss end. Knot the two ends together, then hide the ends.

With Black embroidery floss, embroider eyes on Rnd 9, 6 sts apart in same manner.

BODY

Rnd 1 (Right side)**:** With Tan, make an adjustable loop to form a ring; work 6 sc in ring; do **not** join, place marker.

Rnd 2: 2 Sc in each sc around: 12 sc.

Rnd 3: (Sc in next sc, 2 sc in next sc) around: 18 sc.

Rnd 4: (Sc in next 2 sc, 2 sc in next sc) around: 24 sc.

Rnd 5: (Sc in next 3 sc, 2 sc in next sc) around: 30 sc.

Rnds 6-9: Sc in each sc around.

Rnd 10: (Sc in next 4 sc, 2 sc in next sc) around: 36 sc.

Rnds 11-14: Sc in each sc around.

Rnd 15: (Sc in next 4 sc, sc2tog) around: 30 sc.

Rnd 16: (Sc in next 3 sc, sc2tog) around: 24 sc.

Rnd 17: (Sc in next 2 sc, sc2tog) around: 18 sc.

Stuff Body with polyester fiberfill.

Rnd 18: (Sc in next sc, sc2tog) around: 12 sc.

Rnd 19: Sc2tog around; slip st in next sc, finish off leaving a long end: 6 sc.

Weave yarn end through the sts on the last rnd to close ***(Fig. 4, page 46)***; secure yarn, then insert it through the Body and out the beginning ring where it will be attached to the Head; do **not** cut yarn.

LEG (Make 2)

Work same as Body through Rnd 4: 24 sc.

Rnd 5: Sc in each sc around.

Rnd 6: Sc in next 12 sc, (sc2tog, sc in next 2 sc) 3 times: 21 sc.

Rnd 7: Sc in next 13 sc, sc2tog 4 times: 17 sc.

Rnd 8: Sc in each sc around.

Rnd 9: Sc in next 11 sc, sc2tog 3 times: 14 sc.

Stuff Leg with polyester fiberfill.

Rnd 10: Sc2tog, (sc in next 2 sc, sc2tog) 3 times: 10 sc.

Rnds 11 and 12: Sc in each sc around.

Slip st in next sc, finish off leaving a long end for sewing.

ARM (Make 2)

Rnd 1 (Right side)**:** With Tan, make an adjustable loop to form a ring; work 6 sc in ring; do **not** join, place marker.

Rnd 2: 2 Sc in each sc around: 12 sc.

Rnd 3: (Sc in next sc, 2 sc in next sc) around: 18 sc.

Rnds 4 and 5: Sc in each sc around.

Rnd 6: (Sc in next sc, sc2tog) around: 12 sc.

Rnds 7-9: Sc in each sc around.

Stuff Arm with polyester fiberfill.

Rnd 10: (Sc in next sc, sc2tog) around: 8 sc.

Rnds 11-13: Sc in each sc around.

Slip st in next sc, finish off leaving a long end for sewing.

TAIL

Rnd 1 (Right side)**:** With White, make an adjustable loop to form a ring; work 6 sc in ring; do **not** join, place marker.

Rnd 2: 2 Sc in each sc around: 12 sc.

Rnds 3 and 4: Sc in each sc around.

Stuff Tail with polyester fiberfill.

Rnd 5: Sc2tog around; slip st in next sc, finish off leaving a long end for sewing: 6 sc.

Using a wire brush, scratch the tail back and forth to snag the yarn and make it fray and fluff ***(Photo 3)***.

Photo 3

BODY ASSEMBLY

Sew Legs to the Body to be in either a standing or sitting position with the shaping pointing forward. Insert the yarn ends through the Body and out the neck; do **not** cut yarn.

Leaving last 4 rnds of Arms unstuffed, flatten last rnd and sew closed. Sew Arms to Body on the third rnd from the top, placing them at a slight angle towards the front. Insert the yarn ends through the Body and out the neck; do **not** cut yarn.

Sew Tail to Body on fifth and sixth rnd from the bottom. Insert the yarn ends through the Body and out the neck; do **not** cut yarn.

Tie all strands together at the neck, then hide all yarn ends in the Body.

Sew Head to Body, sewing around the edge 3 times; secure and hide yarn end.

CARROT

Rnd 1 (Right side)**:** With Orange, make an adjustable loop to form a ring; work 6 sc in ring; do **not** join, place marker.

Rnd 2: 2 Sc in each sc around: 12 sc.

Rnds 3-5: Sc in each sc around.

Rnd 6: (Sc in next 4 sc, sc2tog) twice: 10 sc.

Stuff Carrot with polyester fiberfill.

Rnd 7: (Sc in next 3 sc, sc2tog) twice: 8 sc.

Rnd 8: (Sc in next 2 sc, sc2tog) twice: 6 sc.

Rnd 9: Sc2tog, slip st in next sc, leave remaining sc unworked; finish off leaving a long end for sewing.

Weave yarn end through the sts on the last rnd; secure yarn, then hide yarn end.

CARROT TOP

Rnd 1 (Right side)**:** With Green, (ch 10, sc in tenth ch from hook) 4 times; join with slip st in ch at base of first sc ***(Photo 4)***.

Photo 4

Rnd 2: (Sc in next 10 chs, skip next sc) around; join with slip st to first sc, finish off leaving a long end for sewing.

Sew the center of the Carrot Top to Rnd 1 of the Carrot. The Carrot can be sewn to the Bunny's hand.

GENERAL INSTRUCTIONS

ABBREVIATIONS

ch(s)	chain(s)
cm	centimeters
dc	double crochet(s)
FPsc	Front Post single crochet(s)
hdc	half double crochet(s)
mm	millimeters
Rnd(s)	Round(s)
sc	single crochet(s)
sc2tog	single crochet 2 together
sp(s)	space(s)
st(s)	stitch(es)
YO	yarn over

CROCHET TERMINOLOGY		
UNITED STATES		INTERNATIONAL
slip stitch (slip st)	=	single crochet (sc)
single crochet (sc)	=	double crochet (dc)
half double crochet (hdc)	=	half treble crochet (htr)
double crochet (dc)	=	treble crochet (tr)
treble crochet (tr)	=	double treble crochet (dtr)
double treble crochet (dtr)	=	triple treble crochet (ttr)
triple treble crochet (tr tr)	=	quadruple treble crochet (qtr)
skip	=	miss

SYMBOLS & TERMS

( ) or **[ ]** — work enclosed instructions **as many** times as specified by the number immediately following **or** contains explanatory remarks.

colon (:) — the number(s) given after a colon at the end of a row or round denote(s) the number of stitches or spaces you should have on that row or round.

GAUGE

Gauge is not of great importance; your project may be a little larger or smaller without changing the overall effect. It is best to use a small hook and tight single crochet stitches. The holes between the stitches need to be very small, making your crochet fabric dense. The stuffing should not stretch the fabric or show through the stitches. Use the size hook needed to achieve a tight gauge.

Yarn Weight Symbol & Names	LACE 0	SUPER FINE 1	FINE 2	LIGHT 3	MEDIUM 4	BULKY 5	SUPER BULKY 6	JUMBO 7
Type of Yarns in Category	Fingering, size 10 crochet thread	Sock, Fingering, Baby	Sport, Baby	DK, Light Worsted	Worsted, Afghan, Aran	Chunky, Craft, Rug	Super Bulky, Roving	Jumbo, Roving
Crochet Gauge* Ranges in Single Crochet to 4" (10 cm)	32-42 sts**	21-32 sts	16-20 sts	12-17 sts	11-14 sts	8-11 sts	6-9 sts	5 sts and fewer
Advised Hook Size Range	Steel*** 6 to 8, Regular hook B-1	B-1 to E-4	E-4 to 7	7 to I-9	I-9 to K-10½	K-10½ to M/N-13	M/N-13 to Q	Q and larger

*GUIDELINES ONLY: The chart above reflects the most commonly used gauges and hook sizes for specific yarn categories.

** Lace weight yarns are usually crocheted with larger hooks to create lacy openwork patterns. Accordingly, a gauge range is difficult to determine. Always follow the gauge stated in your pattern.

*** Steel crochet hooks are sized differently from regular hooks–the higher the number, the smaller the hook, which is the reverse of regular hook sizing.

CROCHET HOOKS																	
U.S.	B-1	C-2	D-3	E-4	F-5	G-6	7	H-8	I-9	J-10	K-10½	L-11	M/N-13	N/P-15	P/Q	Q	S
Metric - mm	2.25	2.75	3.25	3.5	3.75	4	4.5	5	5.5	6	6.5	8	9	10	15	16	19

●○○○ BEGINNER	Projects for first-time crocheters using basic stitches. Minimal shaping.
●●○○ EASY	Projects using yarn with basic stitches, repetitive stitch patterns, simple color changes, and simple shaping and finishing.
●●●○ INTERMEDIATE	Projects using a variety of techniques, such as basic lace patterns or color patterns, mid-level shaping and finishing.
●●●● EXPERIENCED	Projects with intricate stitch patterns, techniques and dimension, such as non-repeating patterns, multi-color techniques, fine threads, small hooks, detailed shaping and refined finishing.

ADJUSTABLE LOOP

Wind the yarn around two fingers to form a ring ***(Fig. 1a)***, slide the yarn off your fingers and grasp the strands at the top of the ring ***(Fig. 1b)***. Insert the hook from **front** to **back** into the ring, pull up a loop, YO and draw through the loop on hook to lock the ring ***(Fig. 1c)***.

Working around **both** strands, work stitches in the ring as specified, then pull the yarn end to close ***(Fig. 1d)***.

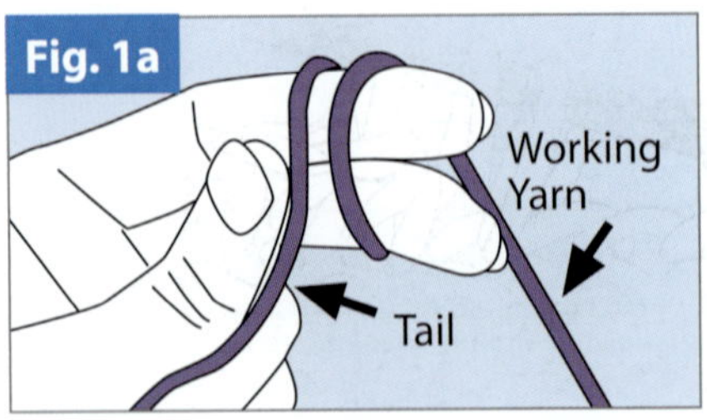

Fig. 1a

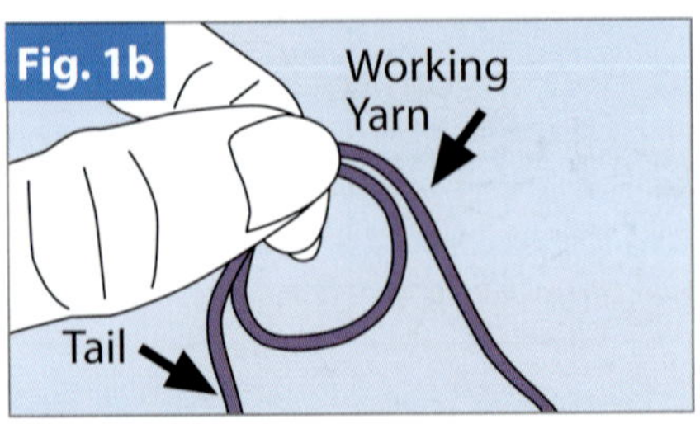

Fig. 1b

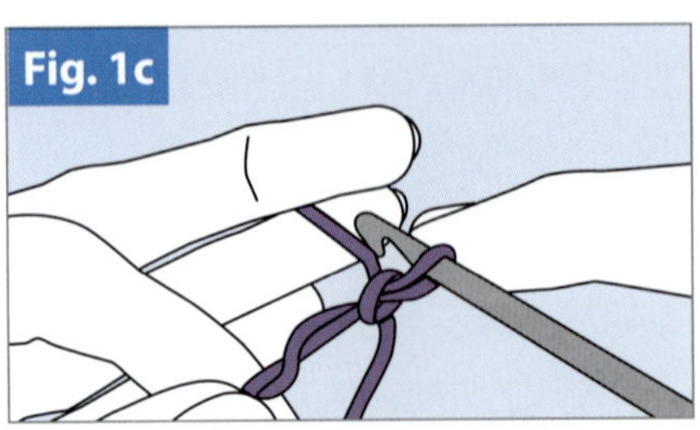
Fig. 1c

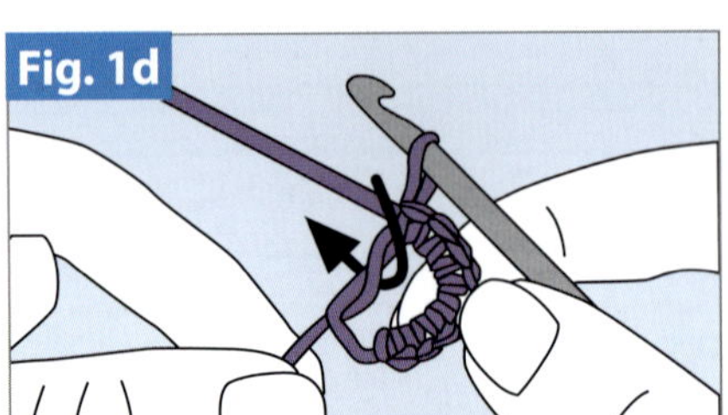
Fig. 1d

TIPS

SAFETY

If the item is for a child that is at risk of choking, do not use buttons or beads as a substitute for the eyes. When using safety eyes, it is important to make sure the eyes are attached correctly by following the directions on the package. Make sure that they can't work their way through the crocheted stitches. When in doubt, embroider the eyes instead ***(see Embroidery Stitches, page 46)***.

STUFFING

Add plenty of polyester fiberfill to the crocheted pieces to maintain the shape, but not so much that it will show through your stitches.

The legs of the standing toys need to be stuffed firmly so that they are stiff enough to hold the weight of the body. Hold each leg as you are stuffing it in such a way as to prevent it from being stretched out of shape.

YARN ENDS

Yarn ends can be inserted into the center of the stuffed parts to hide. Make sure that the yarn used for embroidery is inserted in the center of the piece and doesn't show.

Yarn ends used for sewing should be approximately 10" (25.5 cm) long.

After attaching the Ears to the Head, insert the yarn ends through the Head and out where it will be attached to the Body. Tie all 3 strands together at the neck to prevent any pieces from falling off. Insert all but one yarn end back through Head to hide; pull them tight and cut close to fabric. Use remaining yarn end for sewing the Head to the Body.

Work in same manner for Body, hiding all yarn ends.

MARKERS

Markers are used to help distinguish the beginning of each round being worked. Use a safety pin or place a 2" (5 cm) scrap piece of yarn before the first stitch of each round, moving the marker after each round is complete.

JOINING WITH SC

When instructed to join with sc, begin with a slip knot on hook. Insert hook in stitch indicated, YO and pull up a loop, YO and draw through both loops on hook.

BACK LOOP ONLY

Work only in loop(s) indicated by arrow ***(Fig. 2)***.

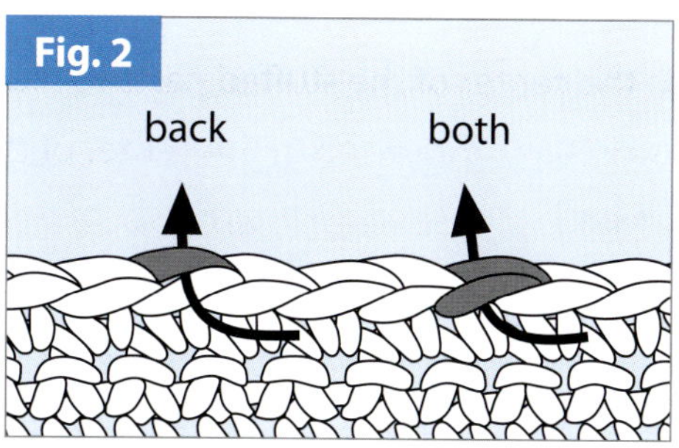

Fig. 2

CHANGING COLORS

Work the last stitch to within one step of completion, drop yarn, hook new yarn ***(Fig. 3a, 3b, or 3c)*** and draw through all loops on hook. Do **not** cut yarn until indicated.

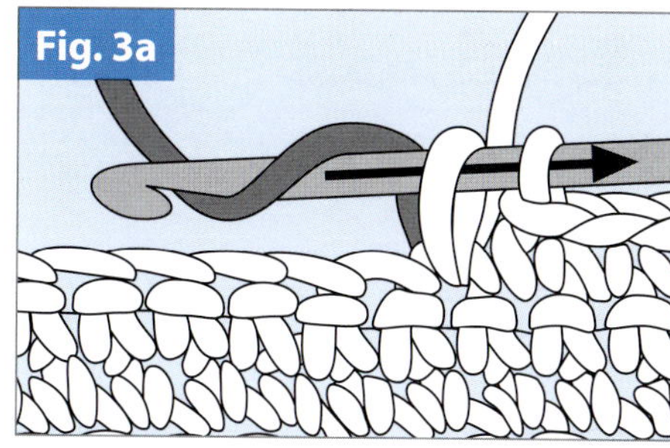
Fig. 3a

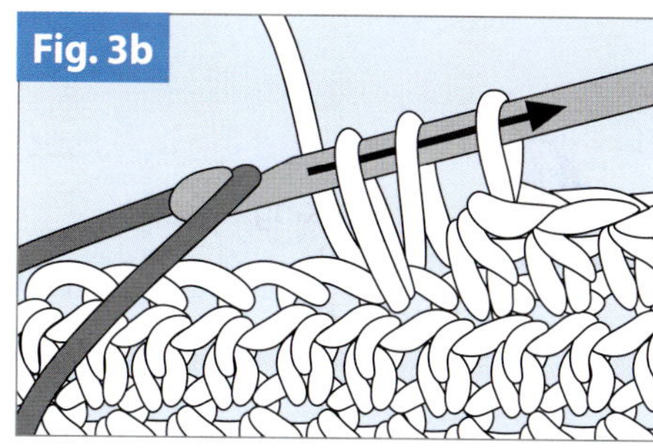
Fig. 3b

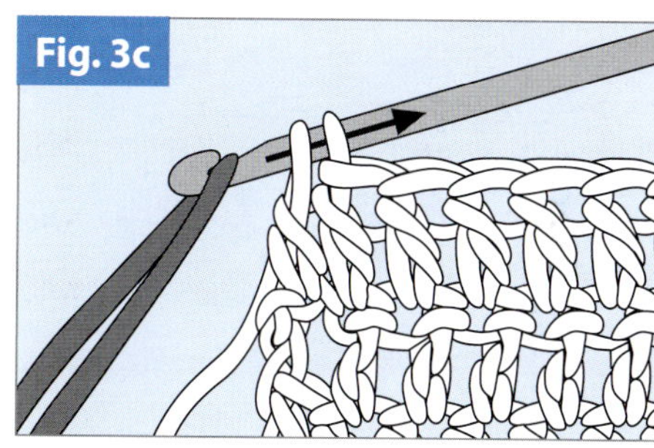
Fig. 3c

WEAVE THRU STITCHES

Weave yarn end through the stitches *(Fig. 4)* and gather to close.

Fig. 4

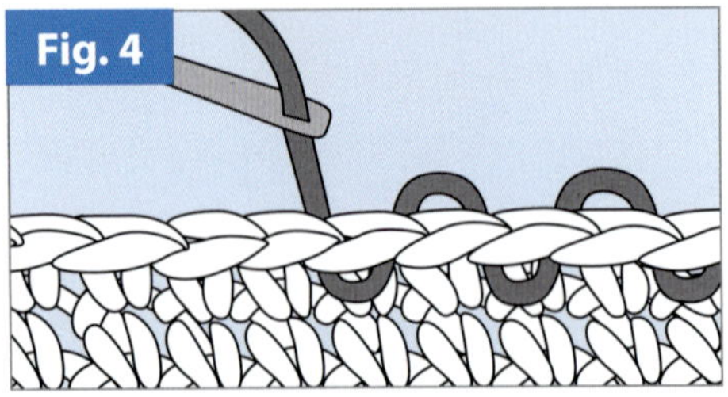

WHIPSTITCH

To sew a piece to another, insert the needle from **front** to **back** through two strands of a stitch **or** end of a row on the top piece, then through a stitch on the bottom piece *(Figs. 5a & b)*. Bring the needle around and insert it through the next strands on the top piece, then through a stitch on the bottom piece. Continue working in same manner.

Fig. 5a

Fig. 5b

EMBROIDERY STITCHES

STRAIGHT STITCH

Straight Stitch is just what the name implies, a single, straight stitch. Come up at 1 and go down at 2 *(Fig. 6)*.

Fig. 6

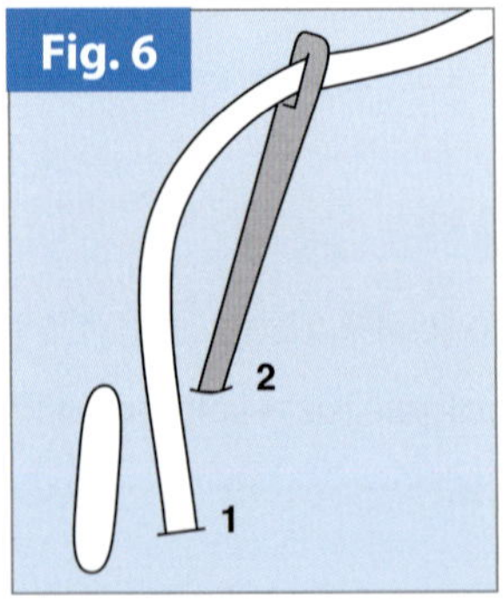

SATIN STITCH

Satin Stitch is a series of straight stitches worked side by side that touch but do not overlap *(Fig. 7a)* **or** come out of and go into the same stitch *(Fig. 7b)*. Come up at odd numbers and go down at even numbers.

Fig. 7a

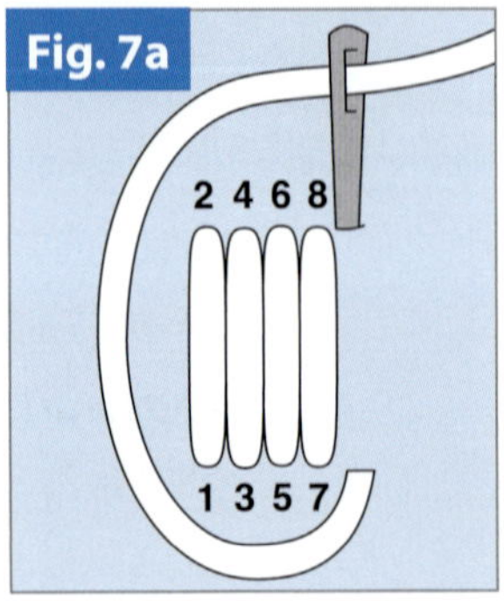

Fig. 7b

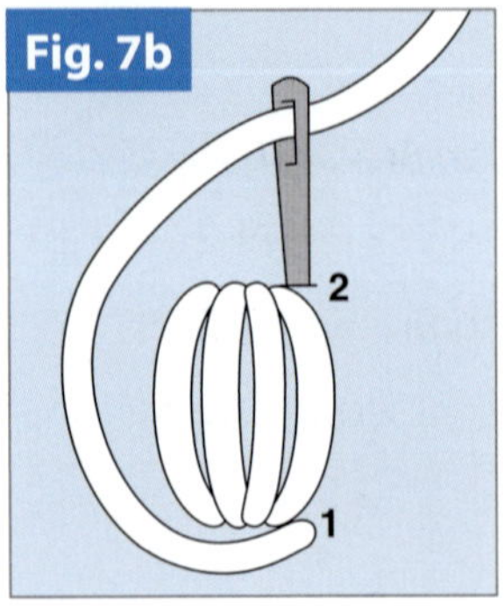

YARN INFORMATION

The items in this book were made using light and medium weight yarns. A bulky weight yarn was also used for the Lamb. Any brand of the specified weight of yarn may be used. It is best to refer to the yardage/meters when determining how many skeins or balls to purchase. Remember, to arrive at the finished size, it is the GAUGE/TENSION that is important, not the brand of yarn.

For your convenience, listed below are the yarns used to create our photography models. Because yarn manufacturers make frequent changes in their product lines, you may sometimes find it necessary to use a substitute yarn or to search for the discontinued product at alternate suppliers (locally or online).

ELEPHANT

Red Heart® Soft Baby Steps®

Light Lavender - #9590 Lavender

Caron® Simply Soft®

White - #9701 White

T-REX

Boy

Lion Brand® Babysoft®

Main Color (Blue) - #107 Bluebell

Caron® Simply Soft®

Contrasting Color (Light Blue) - #9712 Soft Blue

Girl

Lion Brand® Babysoft®

Main Color (Lavender) - #143 Lavender

Red Heart® Soft Baby Steps®

Contrasting Color (Light Lavender) - #9590 Lavender

DUMBBELL RATTLE

Bernat® Softee® Baby™

#30044 Flannel

LAMB

Caron® Simply Soft®

Tan - #9703 Bone

Red Heart® Soft®

Brown - #9344 Chocolate

Lion Brand® Homespun®

White - #300 Hepplewhite

DOLL

Bernat® Softee® Baby™

Grey - #30044 Flannel

Red Heart® Soft®

Skin color - #4601 Off White

Caron® Simply Soft®

Pink - #0015 Strawberry

BLANKET

Caron® Simply Soft®

Color A (Pink) - #0015 Strawberry

Color C (White) - #9701 White

Bernat® Softee® Baby™

Color B (Grey) - #30044 Flannel

TURTLE

Bernat® Satin™

Light Green - #04222 Fern

Red Heart® Super Saver®

Dark Green - #631 Light Sage

Lion Brand® Vanna's Choice®

Green - #171 Fern

Lion Brand® Heartland®

Red - #113 Redwood

TEDDY BEAR

Bernat® Softee® Baby™

Grey - #30044 Flannel

Caron® Simply Soft®

White - #9701 White

Pink - #0015 Strawberry

BUNNY

Caron® Simply Soft®

Tan - #9703 Bone

White - #9701 White

Red Heart® Soft®

Orange - #4422 Tangerine

Lion Brand® Vanna's Choice®

Green - #171 Fern

Meet Tamara Ramsey

Tamara Ramsey enjoys crocheting simple and colorful soft toys for kids of all ages.

"I've been creating soft toys for my own children as well as my friends and family for the past 13 years," she says. Since 2011, she also has been selling her toys and patterns through her website at ostuffandfluff.etsy.com. *Baby's Buddy Amigurumi* is her first book with Leisure Arts.

"I taught myself how to make amigurumi toys from free patterns I found online. After I had made a few, I saw how the basic shapes were made and realized I could alter these shapes to make my own animals."

Bunnies and dolls are her favorite projects. "I tend to find a yarn color I like and then build a pattern around it. My kids help me a lot, too! They give me ideas for new animals, and they help me decide what details should be added."

When it comes to crocheting amigurumi, she encourages people to just have fun. "If your row gets off by a stitch and then does not work out right, it's OK!" she says. "Crochet is very forgiving, and you can easily add another stitch or decrease a stitch and keep going. It's supposed to be fun, not stressful. Being off by a stitch or two will not change the look of your pattern. I know the child who cuddles your toy will never notice! The important thing is to enjoy creating something and have fun."

Tamara works on her crochet projects in the evenings, after home-schooling her three children during the day. She and her husband recently finished Bible college and began work as pastors of their first church.

We have made every effort to ensure that these instructions are accurate and complete. We cannot, however, be responsible for human error, typographical mistakes, or variations in individual work.

Production Team: Instructional/Technical Editor - Cathy Hardy; Editorial Writer - Susan Frantz Wiles; Senior Graphic Artist - Lora Puls; Graphic Artist - Leia Morshedi; Photo Stylist - Lori Wenger; and Photographer - Jason Masters.